Forbidden Scriptures

ALSO BY BIODUN ABUDU

Tales of My Skin

Stolen Sanity

Forbidden Scriptures

A Collection of Erotic Poetry

Biodun Abudu

www.BiodunAbudu.com

Copyright © 2020 by Biodun Abudu
All rights reserved

Printed in the United States of America. No part of this book may be used or reproduced in any manner whatsoever without written permission except in the case of reprints in the context of reviews.

Art Work Concept : Biodun Abudu
Graphic Illustration : Henry Jimenez

ISBN-13: 978-1-7335910-2-7

For the sexually open minded individuals who are on a journey to feel the endless power.

Forbidden Table of Contents

1. Into My Scriptures ………………..… 1
2. Making Love for Dinner …………..…..4
3. All About Me……………………….….8
4. Untitled ……………………………….10
5. Big Break…………………………..……12
6. Upgrade ……………………………....14
7. Yummy Yum……………………..……16
8. Pussy Power……………………..……18
9. Drive Thru…………………….…..20
10. Penis and Pickles………………...…..22
11. Wall Art Exhibition………………...24
12. Belle of The Ball…………………..……26
13. Ouch Station (69th Street)……..……28

14. Private Petals…………………..….…..30

15. Connect the Cherry Dots…………..32

16. Path of Pleasure…………………….34

17. Business Center……………………..36

18. My Mission Statement ……………38

19. Virtual Vending Machine………….40

20. Cyber Pleasure……………………..42

21. Phone Bone…………………………44

22. Daddy ATM…………………………48

23. Sextasies……………………………..50

24. Eclipse………………………….……52

25. Underneath the Sheets…………...….54

26. Just a Dominatrix Thing……….…..56

27. Tour Guide……………………….…..60

28. Holy Foreplay………………….……62

29. Wet Lady Garden……………....…..64

30. Sweat, Tears and Cum………….…..66

31. Genie in the Bottle…………………68

32. On My Backside……………………70

33. Black Booty Gum………………...…72

34. Pure Addiction ………………...…74

35. Our Dance…………………………..76

36. Spring Time…………………………78

37. Early Hunting………………………80

38. Weed McMuffin……………………82

39. Condoms……………………………84

40. Guys r' us……………………………86

41. My Way…………………………...88

42. Countdown 4 Sex…………………..90

43. One Mission………………………..92

44. My Satisfying Fan…………………94

45. Fantasy World………………………96

46. Most Wanted Puppet……………….98

47. My Back Mansion…………………100

48. Got Dick ?……………………………102

49. Invest In It……………………………104

50. My Booty Box…………………..……..106

51. Rated XXX……………………………108

52. The Healing Machine……………..110

53. Guaranteed Pleasure………………112

54. Pussy Bubble Pop………………….114

55. Sex for Breakfast…………………..116

56. My 12D Booty………………....118

57. The Booty Fountain……………….120

58. My Sex is Like……………………..122

59. Chew Me Up………………………124

60. Freak or Treat……………………..126

61. Locked and Loaded……………….128

62. Just a Dream………………………130

63. Pleasure Chest…………………….132

64. The Moist Prophecies for Sexual Scriptures ……………………………..134

65. The Confessions of a Sinful Capricorn……………………………………..138

Pleasure is a journey to continuously enjoy the ultimate satisfaction.

Passion is an endless story that we never can put a full stop to.

Pain is pleasure and is a necessary role in our sexual journey.

Power is freedom and is a major part of a sexual awakening.

Into My Scriptures

(Featured in the novel "Stolen Sanity" written by Biodun Abudu)

My nipples are like two heavenly antennae that should be given proper acknowledgment. It's the rightful thing for you to get on your knees before my altar. Stick your tongue between my two chapters, feel free to support your movement with your hands setting them apart like the Red Sea. My moaning and humming are the chapters in the new era that could be quoted for salvation.

The writings on my thighs represent the times you have signed in and signed out for your passionate shift and have piped me down tremendously. At this moment, I want you to come into thy temple. Conquer my body and pin me across the wall. Shatter my pillars and cast away my doubts.

Administer your potential into my body, let my waterfall dispense down my thighs and unto the marble floor.

Forbidden Scriptures   Biodun Abudu

Making Love for Dinner

After a long hard day at the construction site
I surrender to you

You can tap me on the shoulders so I can
roll on over to you

I already have been tossing and turning and
my sexual hunger has already been growing

Let's make our bodies begin to connect together and create an intimate bond

I bet by the time we are done the perfect wet
dream will flow in

I want to love you so bad, sitting on your horizon
while my eyes set upon the full moon

Then I'll close my eyes because I know by the sun
rise I'll feel so sore but so good

Forbidden Scriptures   Biodun Abudu

The intense volcano heat we produce won't let me exhale at all with sweat dripping down my back

I still enjoy every second you take slowly in me to satisfy my every need

You do it so well I have to threaten you to never ever stop and keep going hard

You're the reason I have an energetic glow when I'm at work or amongst my friends

Follow me into this dimension that your tool has taken me to mentally, as you knock on my wet walls

Take charge of me because that's the role you were meant to play with aggression

Till death do us part you keep me warm inside with your endowment and from the cold nights with your body heat

In sickness and in health, I'm happy in your arms regardless of how sore my three holes are

Forbidden Scriptures   Biodun Abudu

For better and for worse I know you'll keep making love to me until I take my last breath on this earth

Forbidden Scriptures   Biodun Abudu

All About Me

Entice me with your endowed piece of art
Hold my waist and then squeeze my neck
Guide me with your fingers across my thighs
Scan my body with your super vision

Captivate me with your new and exciting positions
Stimulate me with your tongue lingering between my thighs
Set me free with your deep penetration
Pound me with your unique master tool

Make me yours by grabbing and pulling my hair
Trust me with a kiss on my soft lips
Criticize me by spanking me on my cheeks
Bend me over with your sexual experience

Keep me warm from within my wet walls
Carry me to the roof top to knock down my walls
Soak me entirely with your creamy nutrients
Then smile at me to give me assurance for another possible round

Forbidden Scriptures   Biodun Abudu

Untitled

Like the skies, it's here to stay everyday
Like a thief in the night, it can come unexpectedly from the back
Like a shooting star or meteoroid, it can move really fast
It brings a smile upon a man or woman's face
It makes a person at times speechless
It seems like a spell when you do things you have never done before for it
Sadly enough, it ruins people's life sometimes
It's very nice when going in but can be mean when it enlarges and becomes rough
It's very light but when it grows it weighs in pounds
It's something that is celebrated amongst curious girlfriends who are wondering about your sudden glow
It turns my box into a fountain of water flowing endlessly

Big Break

It's part of the law that after four hours you take a break
So, I suggest you head home from work during this break
A text on your phone will explain the path to your big break
You have my full attention, ready in my own bedroom wide awake

At the door is the key to the house let yourself in to my mansion
Take off your work uniform clothing to release your tension
I want you totally fully naked to begin our world cup session
Take a step into my warm wet mother land dimension

Take an easy access to speed the process of this amazing pleasure
However, be steady to grip on to me as a frame to frame picture
Take charge of my power circuit and begin to work my fixture
Get lost in my jungle park and explore my wild but tight nature

Please look into my eyes as you bless me slowly with your lips
It such a pleasure that you're in my territory giving me monumental deep dips
I commend you on your fulfilled million- dollar accomplishment
Your break time is over but I really think you should work from home

Upgrade

From a little pen to a thick baseball bat
Under me like a bedsheet
Concentrating on feeding your hole
Kicking in new and exciting positions

Me and you could have amazing moments together
Enough to provide you a waterfall

No is never an answer for us
On top of the ladder of satisfaction
Whenever, wherever, however I'll be there

Forbidden Scriptures	Biodun Abudu

Yummy Yum

In and out is the process
Mild and wild is the speed
Faded like smoking weed
Now follow my lead to success

Open wide give me every access
Splitting you apart like the Red Sea
Body to body and as one, like milk and tea
Crashing into you, relieving your stress

Keeping your body busy like the big Apple
Marking my territory in your private pond
Rocking you out as you wet the marble floor
Doing a drive by on your nipple

Splash, splash, in your private pond
Leaking and soaking up the marble floor

Pussy Power

Powerful Gem
Ultra pink
Sacred treasure
Sensual power
Your entrance to the world

Precious particulars
One of a kind
Wonder land
Earned Rewards
Royal property

Forbidden Scriptures   Biodun Abudu

Drive Thru

Pulling up on you around 2 a.m. or 3 a.m.
Walking into your unlocked secret door
With you already in position
Your nipples, your lips are on the menu
Moist options, soft selections, edible layers
I'll order a super- sized triple special meal
Your mouth, your fat cakes and your kitty
All of which are going to keep my tool warm
Giving you 5 stars for a pleasurable fulfillment
As you provided me the best meal ever

Penis and Pickles

I used to chat with someone whose screen name was "dick and donuts" and every time we chatted I wished his dick poked me through my glazed donut hole till he oozed out some cream filling from his magic stick. Whenever I came across the words Cucumbers and cocks, I remembered his Cock which was thick like a fat cucumber that I usually picked up from the grocery store.

When we met it took 45 mins for him to peel off my layers, visualizing my dimensions right before he proceeded to invest in my private company. He was experienced at eating my fat/plump ass like a cupcake giving a whole new meaning to the words "cupcakes and ass". Oh, Pussy and Peaches thou art perfect together. In his own words, My Pussy was juicy and wet like a peach that's been bitten into whenever he went downtown on me.

My nipples were sweet like litchi and it's there he made my body a fruit salad using his tongue, lips and teeth if needed.

Forbidden Scriptures　　　　　　　　Biodun Abudu

Wall Art Exhibition

You are cordially invited to my art show
Make your way into my private gallery
New, creative and exciting positions have been selected for this show
Now let me guide you through my private gallery

Tonight, my body and soul are an exhibition
Access my inner and outer layers on display
Feel on my skin, you have my permission
I'm here for you, I will do anything you say

Everything on display is available for you
Work me out starting with my luscious lips
Level up, level up and place me on top of you
My private parts are so juicy you might need a bib

Touch the sky upon the testimony of receiving the greatest pleasure
When you leave my private gallery go ahead and testify
Spread the word about how you had my legs in the air like a bird in the sky

Forbidden Scriptures					Biodun Abudu

Belle of the Ball

Belle of the ball
Beast of the night
Exciting for the night
Perfect for a ball

Shook by the size
He said have no fear
Hanging from a chandelier
The Pleasure of life

Kitty on his mouth like liquor
Kept me humming and moaning
Exciting positions to remember

Memories to last forever and ever
His majesty went in and out till morning
I just wonder if I will ever recover

The end

Forbidden Scriptures   Biodun Abudu

Ouch Station (69th Street)

I'm waiting for a very long train
I am here salivating upon its arrival
Wondering if it will cause me pain
Wondering if I need a guide to survival

The built- in power engine is massive
It's an endless satisfaction from beyond
The speed at which it moves is impressive
A high power going to infinity and beyond

A modern engine touching my inner dimension
Switching tracks constantly, driving in my tunnel
Pain with pleasure, passion that releases tension
Accommodating this train as it drives into my tunnel

My steel wheels screech just as I quickly press the brake
The engine oil leaks making a mess due to my mistake

Private Petals

Step into my private garden of sexual stimulation

Deep in the valley of sensuality, pain and truth

Visually feed your eyes on my complete naked truth

Take a look at me head to toe, touch me for motivation

Grab me by the stem, aggressively but with passion

Take me from the garden roof top to the lower levels

Upon your sunshine I open wide, I open my private petals

So, you can poke me like a bee to a sunflower on a mission

Placing me in another position that you have appointed

Sprinkle your fresh natural water all over my petals

Letting 40 percent of the water reach deep in my roots

With a finger, check to see if I am thoroughly moistened

Pat it, touch it gently, make it feel extremely special

Remember my petals are delicate like that of a special fruit

Connect the Cherry Dots

Smooth like pancakes on a plate I lay my body down for you

Anticipating your maple syrup to glide down my skin, I lay still

Work me like a 9 to 5 job and grab onto my body like a dollar bill

No one else can operate and work my inner dimensions like you

For a quiet but massive storm I let down my sacred walls just for you

This is a path to pleasure and pain for you to achieve and fulfill

Touch me gently and as I moan it signifies the path for you to fulfill

Forbidden Scriptures   Biodun Abudu

Slowly but surely, we switch positions still focusing my energy on you

Let the taste of my bosom be a new sensation for your taste buds

As you connect the cherry dots with your tongue on my smooth skin

With a finger you can access the temperature between my thighs

In position to get mine I moan; I grab unto you unleashing a flood

Place your American sausage in between my English McMuffin

In the right direction to get yours, you explode in between my thighs

Path of Pleasure

Oh, Ouija board, I call upon you to direct me in the right path of pleasure

Tell me yes or no to these sexcapades I have lined up tonight to execute

Spell out words that will set the level of aggressiveness I am to execute

I am part of a higher entity and that is why I am the very one to truly treasure

Place my soul unto a higher ground as I ride on his penis for my pleasure

Point me to the number of sexual positions I am to practice and execute

Move his fingers from the board to my thighs and keep his lips on mute

Forbidden Scriptures / Biodun Abudu

I am determined to fulfill this mission and to enjoy the ultimate pleasure

In a room filled with multiple players its only right that I continue to reapply

Projecting my thoughts into their minds, placing my body on the next player

I have to say hello to all, since you have taken it upon yourself to oversupply

Capitalizing on the movements in-between my thighs before I say goodbye

Hand movements on my private planchette as I proceed to the next player

After he showers me with his nutrients just then I can say goodbye

Business Center

I think of the business center as the territory for international sextivities

A place where all major condoms are accepted for easy transactions

Where private parts consistently collide for business and social activities

Where all foreplay languages are spoken and practiced in different sections

A man with a master plan can penetrate and touch the top of my tower

I have to assess his growth plan that he submits into my inner walls

My legs will stay up in the heavenly clouds like antennas on a tower

From north to south to east to west he constantly pokes my inner walls

Creating an energy in my blood stream making my nipples super hard

Using all networks and resources available from my mouth to my hand

Measure the heat pressure I am able to endure while you stay rock hard

Creating a smooth business transaction for every inch you have at hand

Once we are done, give full percentage of the proceeds to my upper body

Let it snow, let it rain, let it drip down from my head and down my body

My Mission Statement

My mission statement was to provide the ultimate pleasure

So I, made a target market of nine inches and above

Looking to accommodate all and to satisfy my wet Lisa

My location plan involved all boroughs and zip codes

I had tons of creative ideas and set plans to provide the ultimate pleasure

My competitors were nothing to me because they lacked creativity

All ethnic backgrounds were welcome but I spent more time on the black duties

Operating through phone sex, in a car parked in the alley, in the office and more

Forbidden Scriptures   Biodun Abudu

I wanted to be unique and stand for the words all satisfaction guaranteed

I wanted to connect people to the real deal and give them the best

I wanted to offer great tasting, healthy and juicy wet vagina for all

I wanted to offer great sexual experiences on air and on the ground

Thanks to my growth plan I now moan from the top of the highest mountains

Twitching and shaking from under the sea, giving the most compelling sexual experience

Virtual Vending Machine

A virtual vending machine filled with human snacks

Strawberry, chocolate, vanilla are all intact

Inserting the coin and it gives you a sex siren with a 6 pack

This becomes an addiction that will bring you back

Different shapes and sizes leave you suddenly craving

A taste of the juice and you definitely won't be leaving

In pleasure you dig deep discovering the creamy caramel filling

A pop from the bottle gets your mighty stick pouring

In amazement that new snack is a satisfaction guaranteed

The deeper you bite in, the more you taste what's been buried

You plead for more and more than you can actually take

When you finish you cherish this taste and this memory forever

Cyber Pleasure

Cyber-sex is so intense and so digital

Keyboards are pressed like my body so magical

Wires are connected in and out, deeper and deeper

Instant messaging sounds are made like moans so incredible

The computer loads like a man wearing his condom

The computer has a brand just like a condom has a gold magnum

The computer is delicate so is the little temple that is being pounded on

At times it freezes and at times it's fast like a penis entering the kingdom

The files or folders are placed on different spots on the screen so does it apply in different sex positions on the bed

The loading screen is a hint for ready to cum action and so is the precum that oozes out from when given head.

The browser searching for information till you find the exact one is just like a penis playing in the pool till it hits the right spot

The use of spyware to clean virus is as much as cleaning the body of sex fluids

Phone Bone

It's a confidential phone sex, phonography or simply a phone bone

With a manly but silky moan that form up a hot ring tone

Exchanging dirty, naughty, freaky images through a video phone

In our own world, dimension and imagination its best to be alone

Zippers come down; pants touch the ground because my mouth is coming to town

Telling me how your tool hits my tonsils deep, deeper and all the way down

Wearing the crown as I take pride in fulfilling your every need

Forbidden Scriptures   Biodun Abudu

Think of me spreading myself over the kitchen
counter top and maybe the balcony edge

No sounds till you ram your enormous manhood
into my unique world wide web

I let my hands be useful as we talk about you in-
stalling your premium package

Aim at your target, let your missile hit the spot, let
it hit that soft juiced up web

This dirty talk is erupting a long- kept volcano
about to explode from a broken age

Exhale and take deep breaths as you squeeze on
your baseball bat Mr telephone man

We both are ready and set to start transmission, we
countdown speaking in tongues

Release your fat nut against my chin while I release
my creamy but wet warm creamy juice

Think of it sliding down on your chest and that's the least I can do for you mister telephone man just keep me on speed dial anytime.

Forbidden Scriptures					Biodun Abudu

Daddy ATM

When I heard his status, my pockets began to shiver

When he told me he got promoted, my status got raised

Even when he wanted me wet, he had to make it rain

His money is my pleasure and his empty pocket is my pain

The only languages I speak are in Kuwaiti Dinar, Euro, Dollars and Pounds

The only thing to shut me up is money and I won't even make a sound

I can't accept a single dollar bill; I need something that weighs a lot more

Forbidden Scriptures   Biodun Abudu

A full stack of British pounds will heal my stress and will fulfill my sexual needs

Touching money is like connecting your enormous rod to my precious walls

Change my life and have my shopping receipts looking like phone numbers

Time waits for no man, every second, every minute is a waste of a 12- digit check

The fresh smell of money just has me wanting to finger myself so deep

Money is like a big, thick and long dick, just looking at it makes me extremely wet

Split your fortunes in half and shower me with cash like it's the nutrients from your pipe

When I smell your wealth then you can have me anywhere, anyhow and anytime

I'll be dedicated to making sure your money doesn't waste away in your big, thick bank account

Sextasies (sexual fantasies)

Like the sand on a beach, I couldn't count how many rounds we have gone

Like the flow of water, back and forth he stepped in my temple

Like the speed of light he pounded away for a huge nut

Like the ray of light, I shine so brightly after satisfaction

Like a grand boat cruise, I sail gently to my destination

Like a survivor, I rejoice when my lover sets my back free

Like a Nascar racer, I ride till I reach my finishing line

Forbidden Scriptures   Biodun Abudu

Like the end of days my sex skills remain unpredictable

Like a vending machine, I possessed so many goodies

Like the history channel, my body remains informative

Like a candy shop, I'm all you need to sweeten your taste buds

Like the TV Guide, flip through my private wet channels

Like a wedding hall, walk slowly into my territory till you reach the altar

Like a phone, tap my button and swipe thru my plump cheeks

Like a garden, grab my body parts like the essential tools needed to work

Like an art canvas, swipe your paint brush across my lips and paint my face right after

ECLIPSE

Observing and scanning to fulfill my visual appetite
Salivating and appreciating what's before my presence
Touching and squeezing you like a new gadget
Unzipping and unbuttoning like the cutting of a ribbon at a ceremony

Rock hard, super thick and extra- long like a man of steel
Wet and juicy, like a moist atmosphere
Smooth and edible, like special tasty treats
In and out like you're doing intense labor

Mild to wild destined to snatch wigs
Up and down work me into another dimension
Deep and deeper giving satisfaction guaranteed
Dripping and splashing designated to snatch souls

Underneath the Sheets

Hit my body hard like a meteoroid, hitting earth
Crash and go miles deep into my wet realm
Take away my soul and place my chronicles high
Then let my innocence be missing for life

Letting two generations collide and make history
Let there be an endless story between our bodies
Let us be on our way to conceive an angel
Load up and let go of your home training or manners

Take me to a long and unforgettable place underneath the sheets
Make a powerful statement between our bodies underneath the sheets

Forbidden Scriptures   Biodun Abudu

Just a Dominatrix Thing

Stepping or standing on your neck is my new ultimate pleasure

I like it when I have control over you like I own your soul

Standing over you, leaving your knees bruised up and in intense pain.

Im the type to whip your dad in your absence for my pleasure

Putting my foot in his mouth as he's tied up to my chair

Chains, whips, leather, studs, spikes, cuffs all excite me

Living in sin is the new thing and I have no desire to look back

I find pleasure in punishing your girlfriend by pulling her hair aggressively

Forbidden Scriptures   Biodun Abudu

Smudging her red lipstick before I kiss her and taste her pretty lips

I like it rough and pain is my pleasure with my heels stepping on your cock

Bending over, spreading my cheeks on your face and chocking you with it

Ripping your boxers and bouncing with all my weight really hard on your dick for a few seconds

Motorboating you with no pity and I may give you the opportunity to titty fuck me

Before then I have to get you to worship my feet. Like sniffing and inhaling my red polished nails

Moving on to my favourite festish which is the ball busting

Chocking you while I grind on you in my leather tight one piece suit

You can be powerful in the public eye but in our world you are forever submissive to me and I will hande you anyway I want. You will take instructions from me with no hesitations.

Tour Guide

Let me be your tour guide and show you where to place your fingers
I'll walk you through all the precious wet and sweet tourist attractions
Study my dimensions and my soft and smooth architectural design
Visit my art gallery and walk into my museum and take your time in it

Drive and speed through my historical street lanes and park if needed
Let me provide information and assistance to get your pleasure
Explore different cultures and many organized wet establishments
Make sure you have a rubber when going into these city attractions

HOLY FOREPLAY

Knock on my door like a Jehovah witness
Flip open my biblical scriptures
Part my thighs apart like the Red Sea
Lick my soft sacred private chapters

Put your fingers in between my verses
Pull out your rod and staff so my heavens can open up
Put me on the altar and worship my body
Find redemption in my house of salvation

Go deep in my temple so my river Nile can flow endlessly down my thighs
Continue to build my Tower of Babel so I can speak in different languages
Let there be complete satisfaction at the midnight hour
Perform a miracle so I can be converted to a saved soul

Let your mighty David defeat and tame my little
Goliath
Then let me baptize myself in your creamy nutrients
so I can be anew

WET LADY GARDEN

My wet glands are like the rain forests with a caution sign right before you take a deep splash into my private pool. My juice box is for sure a thirst quencher and can leave you obsessed and whipped. It tastes like a mango tango water fountain that's also a generous slurp central with a strawberry or pineapple taste.

It's an unforgettable wet memory and wet moment. A sacred forever flowing river fall and water spring. It's the legendary river Nile with soft edible layers that spread apart like the Red Sea. So, you can go ahead and embark on a challenging but fulfilling journey through my wet tunnel.

Rain forests
Wet Glands
Thirst Quencher
Private pool
Deep Splash
Pineapple Taste
Juicy Box
Mango Tango
Water fountain
Wet memories / moments
Water springs
River falls
Slurp central
River Nile
Wet tunnel

Sweat, Tears and Cum

In and out goes your magical stick and I cry. You me give me a mild to wild kind of passionate sex and I cry. Your magic stick grows in me, getting bigger and bigger and I cry once again. These tears continue to fall from my eyes to the ground as I cry.

Gliding down my body to your body it's my sweat. I sweat because of our intense work out together. I sweat because of the connection, the sparks and bond between us. I sweat as we both race to the finish line.

As I kneel before you to exercise my mouth I receive an unexpected shower of nutrients from your nut cannon. Flowing down my soft thighs, gliding down my succulent breast, taking a detour on my juice box and passing through my butt cheeks. You my dear give the best definition ever of what it is to really cum!.

Genie in the Bottle

Witness the most precious pussy ever
Pink, tight, soft, juicy so make a wish
Be good and you can have it forever
Admire the details, texture and make another wish

If it's empty you have to rub it
Insert one finger to taste the frequency
Get on your knees, move your face close to it
Blow on it a little more frequently

You will have way more than 3 wishes
This an endless flowing fountain
You will have uncountable wishes
This is a sweet tasting juice fountain

Make it your priority to set my pussy free
Everything you do should be totally hands free

On My Backside

On my backside, I had a mission of searching for quality and not quantity

On my back side was where certificates of street credibility were given to the achievers

My backside could be a manual computer for professional men to work with at scheduled times

My backside was the one and only youthful fountain that's why I stayed naturally juiced up, there was no need for lube at times

On my backside condoms were the only way to go in and out of my heaven

On my backside there was a paradise of fun games to play and rivers of flavors to taste

My backside was associated with the words bubble, plump, firm, tight, smooth, fat

Forbidden Scriptures   Biodun Abudu

Entering my backside was like entering into the hall of fame with only certain words that were spoken but most of all, men just observed with a pure silence of amazement.

My backside was like that million- dollar lottery you win that you can't help but to smile all through going in and out wondering if that moment was just a dream because it was too good to be true.

My backside had men heading towards rehab all because I cut off the wet supply

My backside was all they saw and it was one of the few fabulous diamonds in midst of oil stained industrial rocks.

Black Booty Gum
(Inspired from the novel "Tales of My Skin" written by Biodun Abudu)

Tear my clothes open from head to toe like unwrapping a sweet candy
Putting your head underneath my robe is like peeking into a jar with candy
Find your way through my coated first layer is like a butter scotch caramel filled candy
Making your selection on where to begin our sex is like shopping at a store filled with sweet candies

Sticky is one characteristic of a candy and it is just like a trait of manly oozed warm cum
Sweet is the candy description just like my bubble ass when you rim it to get you some
Many high priced flavors are provided at my African candy galore stand
Rubbing your tongue against a candy could be like soaking my body with your tongue

Pure Addiction

Seeing my body, you need to take caution
So, take heed and follow the precaution
My body in person is the real fun and action
I don't roll with slackers who don't function

All I need is an addition not a subtraction
A baseball bat not a pencil makes a connection
Play in my field and I'll be your addiction
Picture me with you in different scenes and positions

I'll be an unforgettable fantasy and I'll be a great addition
Not a single question, just keep me in your imagination
For you, no need for a registration in my dimension
Do it right, keep it tight, to end at the right destination

Our Dance

The intense sexual movement is like dancing
The penis shakes, twists then cums like its sweating
The ass jiggles, whines enjoying the rhythm of the pounding
The requests of different positions can be quite demanding

A nice ass and a nice dick always meet on the dance floor
The gyrating energy gets out hand from mild to wild and more
Dancing the requiem, the two spirits move in, out, up and down
The serenade is that special movement that gives an easy flow like water

Our shadows become one piece to the tune of nocturne
The massive body heat produces fire as we collide in a bolero dance
We find our way through each other's forest to the step of the minuet

Shinning like the sun is your prelude of intense ray of light in my sight
Finally applauding I give praise to your wonderful routine in my temple of time

Spring Time

Like springtime my petals blossom
Colourfully, attracting lots of manly cum
But I am not young, dumb and full of cum
Massive amounts of passionate sweat keeps me
high like rum

Your pole stings my hole continuously
Like a bee you lay all in me uncountably
Like a lonely flower you grab on me and devour
But every move, every step I enjoy every hour

Taking me down and taking charge in my enjoyable
weakness
I bear the sweet pain from the powerful evolution in
weakness
Injecting a massive destruction releasing pure honey
drops in my weakness
All this in my pleasurable, most grateful, most
speechless weakness

Forbidden Scriptures   Biodun Abudu

Early Hunting

Nothing is wrong with an early morning browsing
Although it's really some early morning hunting
Some hide behind the wall of daily love searching
Still left in self- deception they keep on digging

For me I keep on searching for that goody boy treat
I even advertise my own goodies for anyone to eat
It serves as a give and take hook up when we meet
Most times I call it trade by batter with plenty to eat

I want my body to be attached to him like hands to glove
Hunting that treat will be a problem I will definitely solve
When I find him, he will have access to all of my above
In my dominion he can give a massive push and shove

Even if I don't find him online, I can go out and order
You best believe my good boy treat will be a chocolate or vanilla lover
Once I capture him, he will be mines to discover all over
In fact, I'll leave his body helpless like it was a murder

Weed McMuffin

Can I order a Weed McMuffin, one very hot day I was asked
I could not say no after all its my duty and it's my only task
He got the right tool size and right bass proportion for my tight flask
I hoped his face wasn't anything like a Halloween Freddie mask

Like Brownie weed crumb he seemed so delicious to me
Then the moment came when he bit out of my apple dee weed crumb
He then requested a special order for his friend called de dumb
I hoped he wasn't anything like an overgrown hairy street bum

Caramel weed cake is his favourite flavor and was on my menu
I gave it up in silence when he stretched his hands like rent was due

He drained my elements as I stayed still waiting for chapter two
Suddenly he proposed his own principles with a pinch of fondue

My creamy hole seemed to have his full attention as he was pulling in and out
Enjoying life with all its passionate pleasure he kept on pounding
He paid tribute to my hole leaving his tropical weed slush pouring on my backside
It was as thick as a weed-a nilla shake it made me silently smiling

Condoms

I like to have condom-less sex when I am writing my poems, novels, articles and so much more but when it comes to sex. I will always and forever will stay strapped and protected no matter what that 14.5 inch flavored sweet and sour dick says or whatever that candy sticky strudel booty or pussy does.

For those who still don't understand my internal words I am basically saying I will always will remain faithful to a condom and my trust lies with protected sex. I can be a freak all day and night, month and years with condoms on. You can't enter into a man's magnificent mile or at least the inauguration hall of a woman although I consider it heaven that produces angels, without a condom.

At this stage I will say strapping a condom on is a basic knowledge of a wise man and woman. If you still decide to live by the basis of saying you can't lick a lollipop with the wrapper on then I tell you that your going on at your own risk.

"CONDOM" one word is enough for the wise.

Guys "R" Us

Free loads of men being dropped off online or at the corner

Strong language is executed during interactions with all potential individuals

Sexual situations always take place whenever and wherever

Violence may occur only maybe when the dick beats the pussy

I go through guys at this store like money flying out my hands

In fact, the boys at this store just come and go like every season

Sexing a man from this store is like putting my socks on everyday

Forbidden Scriptures · Biodun Abudu

I had sex so many times like uncountable sea sand when I visit

Needing a man for me is like the basics: food, shelter, clothing

So, if I don't stop at my favourite store the day will feel empty

Some of the men came delivered from out of state right on time

The best part of guys r' us is that the men come free of charge

If I'm in the guys r' us store I'm looking to purchase immediately

There are definitely no refunds at this store it's a one- time deal

Everybody is salivating and bidding to grab the artifact on display

Please note that only the experienced are allowed in guys r' us

My Way

I study men to get a degree on how to spend their money
I take lessons outside of school in order to be called honey
I play sports for skills to touch down or slam dunk in bed
I signed up for the military to be able to fight wars in bed

I studied psychology to be able to mind play with my lover
I have movies like basic instinct for mind games as a cover
I work my way into his wallet and become his commander
I become a protector so I alone can spend his money forever

I write goals and plans that will help me get him on his knees to use his tongue
I plead for his entire existence to manifest itself in all my holes

Forbidden Scriptures — Biodun Abudu

I take every move he makes on my soft skin very serious
I sex him all the time to make a future as he plants his seed

I take the lead so I won't be left alone unsatisfied
I take charge because only me can show him how deep and hard I would like to be penetrated
I get crazy when he nuts way to quick after 10 mins

Which is why I take my time with some foreplay before we get to the main course where my ass claps on his stick

Forbidden Scriptures Biodun Abudu

Countdown 4 Sex

10. With signs of body language the after party is at my body so meet me uninvited

9. Go on, rip my clothes, I want to play a crazy sex and aggressive scene in bed

8. Push me on the bed and tell me how to position myself after all you're in charge

7. To promote a more aggressive slayer, I disobey and wait for that manhandling back to the bed

6. No time for slow passionate sex just ram it in and out as you please, you can see I'm in need

5. I already made it clear there is definitely no red light, not even a yellow light but only a green light

4. Dick me down, crash and burn, hit and run, pound, pound, pound and go deeper

3. Wow, you finally have filled up my cake up with your cream filling

2. I'm leaking and I'm soaking wet with all of me dripping to the floor.

1. Mission complete, countdown is over. Thank you for the fuck, now you may leave and close the door behind you.

One Mission

One mission only needs to be urgently completed

All languages brought my way can be reformatted

All major recognizable condoms are accepted

While all nasty raw plays are definitely rejected

If living in sin is the new thing of the new century

Then you need to take a special trip to my gallery

I'm only here to win you over from your wife Kimberly

I speak the truth and only the real truth so take it, I'm sorry

I'll take you on a journey to explore the real meaning of sex

I'll work you over and over leaving your wife to be your ex

My actions speak louder than my words so let's see what's next

Just a note of advice, bring a month's worth of energy, it's really expected.

My Satisfying Fan

My concert is at your house, and I will be performing on you and only on you
My lyrics is about make me your spouse, only because I'm trying win you
My strip- tease is to get you aroused and my mission is to please you, just you
I pass on this pleasure in my most truthful pure connection from me to you

Our moaning and grinding together makes a very sweet musical harmony
The bed rocking sound is the perfect beat and a great intense melody
My body smacks against yours in accordance, completing our desired fantasy
Our sweat soaks my sheets, dripping from our bodies in pure serenity

May I say it was a pleasure to have enjoyed the few hours with you
Just in case it was a one- night stand even though I really would like more

Thank you for pleasing me though it really should be a continuing job for you
And I can't let you go without letting you know, that without you I can't be satisfied, for you are my one and only satisfying fan

Forbidden Scriptures   Biodun Abudu

Fantasy World

Let me pick a sexual fantasy and make it dirty hope
you're man enough to work off the sweat

If you ask of erotic pleasure, I'm the champion, I
hope you're a fifty- minute man to work
my sweat

Don't test me at all because once you get in, there is
no way out, it's a go hard or go home scene

Begin to venture in my fantasy and take a memorable tour of the wonderful gift my body brings

Carry me up gently and spread my thighs right on
the bathroom sink

Fuck me so deep right in front of a three -cornered
standing mirror frame

Lift me up in the air over your head as you dive
your face in between my cheeks

Forbidden Scriptures   Biodun Abudu

Place me on the open balcony rail so that the neighbours can take a peek

Leave your dick sleeping in my tight ass all through the night

Let your dick brush my teeth and your cum showers me in the morning light

Pounding my hole with your pole on the stairwell so intense and so fast

Handle me in the shower like a prison scene using soap and water as lube

Hump me in the boot of the car leaving it open so I can scream louder than the booming speakers

Lock me up with you in a phone booth closely so we can sweat it out, take charge like a leader

Like an ice cream melting down a crispy cone let me lick the pre cum of your enormous stand

Let us breathe in the fresh of air of the beach while we fuck then relax on the beach sand

Most Wanted Puppet

Insert the token and let me scream like a man

Slap my ass and let me cry like a new- born

Pick me up and let me show what I've got

Check my bar code and let me show you my cost

Hurry up and take me home, I already have batteries included

Fondle with my body so I can show you my happy reaction

Press me in the right places so I can gradually get familiar with your touch

I'm so fragile so handle me with care because it's only fair as it may be my first time

Many of my kind are in stock but I'm different, be aware of how you access my dimension

Most are made but I was created and suitable for your needs

You can grab me by the neck or by my waist because I'm so easy to lift up

My underwear can be pulled down or can be pulled to the side.

There are no rules or appointments for when you need to relieve your stress

My Back Mansion

I wanna wake up in the morning with your big thick dick in my wide mouth

Let me kiss your lips and smooth sweaty body, while you lay on the couch

I wanna cater to you and treat you right because that's what my love is about

I'll make sure I fix breakfast, so I can keep you in my loop whenever you go out

There is a honey pure connection between us with a futuristic language that I can't translate

In fact, I have a headache at times wondering if you're really the one, I can't help but to debate

I keep trying to hide the freak in me and I can't help but to let it out and I'm sure you can relate

Forbidden Scriptures   Biodun Abudu

Sorry I am selfish when I tease you, leaving your
boxers soaked with precum that I know you hate

I'll love to show you off to the world, since I have
found such a wonderful unique, discovery and creation

I am not afraid of who I am now, you have given
me a reason to be comfortable in my skin did I mention?

One of my big dreams has always been to accommodate your big piece, yes, I'm talking about your
large nation

Lastly, I am glad you have given me a chance and
for that I assure you a peaceful home in my back
mansion

Forbidden Scriptures Biodun Abudu

Got Dick?

Monday, I put out job ads for someone who has girth and length or inches that can handle me and stretch my pretty holes

Tuesday, I head to the local bar. I scan around the room looking for a potential pipe and not just any pipe but one that can ruin my life

Wednesday, I visit the gym and watch the big dick prints in sweat pants and shorts flapping up and down just imagining how it would feel in me

Thursday, I visit a glory hole to exercise my mouth on anonymous large dicks. Seeing nothing but dicks through the holes just excites me.

Friday, I head over to a sex party and spread my legs wide open on a pool table and watch as some players slide in me till it reaches my tummy. Then I turn on all fours and wait for the other players to bungee jump in my walls till I can't take no more

Saturday, I look back as I sit on him and look at how far I have cum upon his mamba. I have to be proud of myself for taking over his kingdom

Sunday, I would have been praying for my sins but obviously I'm still trying to see who got dick for me and luckily the cable man is on the menu and eager to offer me his enormous black pipe. Hallelujah !!!!

Invest In It

I speak all languages giving fellatio, blow job or
oral sex as long as you can handle it
All races are welcome but make sure the tool is big
enough to dip in
I'm the definition of freaky and I can satisfy you, so
hush and put your dick in it
I ride it so good you may have a chemical reaction
to hit the speed and go for it

My back pillow feels good that you can't help to
finish the good deeds and pat it
My satisfaction is way too much that you have to
put a stop sign or red light in it
Can I spread my gallery open for you to inhale me
and breathe with your nose in it
You play in my historical art museum and how
about you put your signature in it

Don't be scared to put the pleasure where it belongs
and pain can find its way in it
Don't take it for granted but respect and carefully
handle it while you fuck with it

Don't be afraid to jiggle my treasure hole to see
how good your pillar will fit in it
Hit me balls deep in the back as you please then you
can rest while I pray on it

You can beat it on up and then you can softly blow
the wind and get to cooling it
Play a memorable moment while you skeet, squirt,
jerk off and spit the milk in it
It feels good like some famous basket baller just did
a 3- point shot dunk in it
Such a good feeling that I suggest you come back,
make a profit and invest in it

My Booty Box

Many men from all over come anticipated highly
energetic like I am some kind of super bowl
They even leave their lifetime jobs to plead allegiance once they have seen my ass, so dam fowl
My sex game is called kinky, my nick name is even
freaky just a power buttom for dicking
You can surely assist and make me wet as you tease
my fat apple butt getting ready dicking

You can press play on my booty box giving you that
satisfaction as I scream out loud
Let me put my finger in my mouth and pull out to
touch and tease your smooth dick cap
Let pre cum drip on me then I will lick your first fat
nut
We can go on to the next scene because part one is
rap

Insert your huge diamond in my jewelry box so I
can keep you warm like a honey bun
My ass will clap on your dick and it will be such a
nice sight

It's only been two hours and you have already starting leaking
Your dick is spitting come let me chew your nut, hmm taste so good like a bubble gum
Since there is no lube you can release your honey cum in my ass for the next person to get a fuck

I think I want to get it good maybe one, two or three 13- inch dicks in at once
Once you all are inside, you can hit me hard, I mean ram it in heavy like a monster truck
Let me be drenched in a shower of cum leaving my ass hole wide open like I have been fist fucked
Such an outrageous feeling got you squirting cum so much and so fast like your peeing

RATED XXX

I got a fat booty that walks and plays its own unique role
So, I guess I gotta copyright it before I get more swole
I have African lips that slurps and keeps you from a frost- bite
Rated XXX because it's a struggle trying to get in because I'm so tight

I'm so tight that you gotta beat it up leaving me for a hospital check in
Don't be such a pussy I can take it like a dam fucking man so ram it all in
I can't stop the fact that men keep me as a professional referral
Men travel across the globe to get healed by my bailey's caramel

Open up wide I even got some more coming to quench your thirst
When I squirt, it's like a fire hose and they suddenly don't know how to act

My sex game is crazy they said the porn industry looking for me
Super value meal, all you can eat button special but it ain't for free

My dick taste better than a lollipop and its filled with a cream filling in the center
Fondle with my control panel units and you will have something to remember
Keep me in your chapter, in fact, teach me nasty tricks to keep me around to stay in your future to be a part of your history
I will be available in the historical museum with my special booty fossils on display for you to taste

The Healing Machine

My ass is the world's undiscovered tool that can fix the economy
So put your force field dick in like you studying some geometry
10- inch, 13- inch maybe a 14- inch and I'll say yes to diversity
Is it doggy style ? is it pyramid style? what the fuck is your strategy?

I ride it so good, I suck it so nice I guess I'm just blessed with creativity
I keep you coming back, I keep my booty tight, and yep I got persistency
I may have fucked with him but not with your crew and of course I keep accountability
My African features and my many tricks keep me as the most wanted by the porn industry

Exercising your dick and gaining experience is the new way into my walls
So come to me with newly added features like a new technological gadget

Now listen time waits for no man so begin to pump hard and make some productivity
My sex plain and simple is the healing machine so follow the trend, digest and practice my theory

Guaranteed Pleasure

My erotic and passionate sex is like NOKIA (connecting people)
My body or should I say my ass is like PEPSI (ask for more)
My sex drive is very high and so I say like NIKE (just do it)
My body is that fantasy ride so like COCA COLA (Enjoy)

My backside is like ALL STATE insurance so (you are in good hands)
I want you to dominate me and treat me like BURGER KING (have it your way)
I can't help but to have you come to my PLAYSTATION and hit my X BOX so deep
I know for a fact that after our sex I will feel like MCDONALDS (I'm loving it)

Inspired by the online phrase written by an unknown writer "I want you to come over to My SPACE and I'll TWITTER your YAHOO Till you GOOGLE all over my FACE BOOK"

Pussy Bubble Pop

Please breed my pussy and fill me up with nut

Let me stretch back relax and squirt out your nut

No hands just dive your face in and eat me out

It feels so right that I can help but to scream out

In fact, that's not enough slide your dick back in

Take it slow going in and look in my eyes deep in

Once your all in, pull out and go at full speed in me

Let me feel the expansion that my passage deserves

Closed legs don't get fed, so make a statement in between my legs

Take away my innocence and I will always welcome you with an open mouth, open legs and open arms

I'm grown and I can handle all you give to my pussy

Make a pop right in my dimensional 3D pretty pussy

Choke me, hit my walls side to side, in and out, you're in charge

I shouldn't have to tell you how to make me cry for a break

Step into my light its official that I'm about to explode

1, 2, 3 go ! then eject while I erupt my cream filling in codes

Sex for Breakfast

Sausage is a meat that I love to have all in me

They are tasty and fit perfectly right in me

Pour Maple syrup all over me like I'm your pancake

I am ready to go and don't care about work now

Take me now into a graphical section of sexual lust

Toast my soft B buns and insert your sausage in me

I'm asking if you need some butter upon your lips

I can make it less salty and more sweeter with your approval

I'm so hungry that I think ill just eat you out another hour

Making sweet love my milk mixes with your cocoa puff

My strawberry cream and honey drip has begun to pour

If feels right that we have been eating without a plate

I almost forgot to cut some banana slices upon your cereal

I enjoy tasting you and you tasting me right back like that

Lets get wasted early this morning with your french latte

What is a breakfast without your milk pouring on me

My 12D Booty

You can enter my dimension where there are no limits at all

You can play, finger and squeeze on my 3- dimensional ass

You can pump me so hard and watch me nut like a fire hose

You listen to my bussy burb like it's reporting "roger that"

Imma ride you good with pride like I'm sitting on top of the world

Imma let you eat my ass but I hate to see you end up in an asylum or rehab

Imma let you use your dick in my mouth then get to work in another hole

Forbidden Scriptures　　　　　　　　　Biodun Abudu

Imma have to put an insurance on my booty when it turns to a 12 dimensional ass

Take a deep dip into my assculator, while I take you up to different levels and heights

Keep it coming, keep it going like a tread mill because I wanna see you over flow

I need you to solve my problems, so I expect for you to bring the big solution

I hope you can deliver that expensive shuttle pipe well so I can take a trip off to outer space

The Booty Fountain

When you see my body, You can't help but to let your dick say attention
Then when I see it rise up to perfection, I can't help to assume the position
Push my back to arch and bend like you're having some sort of cruel intention
Once you're in me you can calculate the dynamics of my walls like taxation

Once you taste my academy award winning ass you have to keep on ordering
I will let you test the drive, in fact, take the wheels, but please don't be fumbling
The neighbours have already known your name since we have been making hits
How about I sign you to my label and you can leave me a signature with your nut

My sex is the utmost pleasure, that you can't help but to handle with care
I'll put it on you slowly and post online for the whole world to take lessons and rate

Forbidden Scriptures — Biodun Abudu

My booty is like that candy bar you want to grab and take a bite from to taste the cream
I'll make you feel so damn good that you will report the discovery of the booty fountain

Must I remind you that I am the new centuries' definition of great passion sweaty sex
So how about we end this chat and get to tearing each other's clothes
There is only one image with best quality and history's known originality of today
You dare not ask me because my booty is the definition of a dimensional asset with texture

My Sex is like………

My sex is like the discovery channel's most unknown difficult unsolved mystery and up to date

My sex is like a basketball game you dribble, I bounce till you take a 3- point dunk of nut

My sex is like a menu simply irresistible, you keep ordering for more even when you're sore

My sex is like a time travel journey that you wouldn't even know when it has been 12 hours

My sex is like a car race, I keep riding and you go at full speed till we pass the finish line

My sex is like a car repair store, you're pounding me and your oil is leaking from my hole

My sex is like a number 1 single that you can't help just to love it every day

Forbidden Scriptures   Biodun Abudu

My sex is like pirate's mission you put your tool in me to hit my walls hard to find gold

My sex is like being star struck and it leaves you absolutely speechless and in amazement

My sex is like family reunions, its filled with joy as my ass and your dick reconnect again

My sex is like the business center, where business happens between your 13- inch and my fat ass

My sex is like that famous historical museum, that you take a tour and take pictures after

My sex is like Hollywood, there is a lot of sweating, moaning and of course the unexpected action

My sex is like outer space, it has no limits to where it can be done, in the water or on top of the plane

My sex is like the Super Bowl, lot of condoms and lube are present and I'm ready to begin the game

My sex is like a Mardi Gras carnival, so I hope I'm not too freaky to say everyone's invited

Chew Me Up

I want you to chew me all up in complete honesty like a bubble gum

Do me another favour and soak my ass like a water park summer fun

I hope to finally relax to get me loose and high with a bottle of rum

We are just beginning and definitely not at all ready to even cum

Just to dive in my oochie coochie, pussy wussy and get so lost in it

If you aren't beating it up then there is no adventurous fun in it

I want the taste of my yum yum to melt in your warm mouth

Forbidden Scriptures							Biodun Abudu

You can lick it any way you like north, west, east and south

I want to emphasize my lips against the head of your dick

However I hope you take your time in me as the time ticks

I may become very verbal if I feel the need to salute you

It is just me or I'm already leaking and soaking up the sheets

You have it that good that I am hooked upon your tool

Ill take the right caution to ride you till I'm totally full

Full of nut, full of sweat, full of manly tension against me

I have you scheduled for the night so begin to satisfy me

Forbidden Scriptures Biodun Abudu

Freak or Treat

With different sexy customs and different candy body treats

It's either you're in or you're out because our body has to meet

I as well have to deliver my package while you're in position

Be a misses hunter to your tool or you can be a mister pumper to my wall

It only gets better when I play the sweet and innocent one

Then it gets kind of rated xxx when I play the sexual one

I can as well still get off even if you play the brutal one

Forbidden Scriptures   Biodun Abudu

No need for a Halloween party when I'm the happening one

The horror dwells in me when I make a soda can disappear in my mouth

I really want you to be lost in my body deep with no sounds

I do want you to murder my wet walls and create a crime scene

In fact, I want you to squirt a foggy thick cloud and blind my vision

No one else is invited or it will be a total murder scene

You are mine and only mine, no one else can have access to you

I will put a special cast on them called brutality blessings

No one comes in the middle of my freak or treat sessions with you

Forbidden Scriptures — Biodun Abudu

Locked and Loaded

I want you to grab me tightly like a plier tool let me shout

Pound me in like a hammer to a nail and give me a blackout

Give it to me daily so your tool can grow like a bean sprout

If you fail to give me the painful pleasure then I'm heading out

Stay put in the holy temple and never pull your tool out of me

Forever and ever I say onto you as you flow in my inner me

For I have finally come back to my own roots Mister Africa

Forbidden Scriptures

Biodun Abudu

I salute you and bow before your majesty, I'm bound to Africa

I am rest assured that your grenade launcher is fully equipped

Like a cave just explore me and stay warm my private bed

So why wait for the fantasy when the reality is right in me

A taste of this motherland is forbidden but only for thee

I'm like a playboy mansion and all the bunnies are in me

I'm fully fruited up naturally with a thousand endless seas

Keep searching in me and be ready to solve my mystery

Only history can determine if your future lies deep in me

Just a Dream

I had a dream of having a mansion with a sex dungeon inside of it. The sex dungeon would have the best sex parties ever. At the parties the sex dungeon would have glory holes in the basement. Only the largest, thickest and longest dicks would be inserted into those glory holes. Walking past every fat cock and smiling as I rub each one feeling the mushroom heads or veins on their dicks. Dreaming of the potential each cock has to stretch my mouth wide open and enlarge my pretty tight pussy. This glory hole would have the most desired porn stars in the world for everyone to have fun with.

The sex dungeon would have vending machines for people to purchase items from, on their way home. The vending machines would have dildos in all sizes including rubber fist hands that will be great for personal fisting pleasures. Across the room will be another vending machine that will have used under wears from men and women with cum stains or pussy juice upon request.

There will be fun tricks going on along the stairway like seeing a woman using her pussy to smoke a cigarette. Seeing a man or woman making a soda can disappear in his or her mouth. Couples hanging from the chandelier having passionate sex while drops of their sweat hit the ground.

There will be a long hall way with doors and at each door there will be a man or woman or a couple waiting for the invited guest to select them for a wonderful night. Each room will have knee spreaders, whips, chains and more. It will also have the option of broadcasting their session for the singles in the lobby to jerk off to or finger themselves to. There will be men and women dressed in different lace and leather costumes to come clean up the mess made in the lobby.

Pleasure Chest

Pussy galore
Ultimate pathway
Sacred temple
Secret passage
Yummy and pretty

Assteriors
Smooth buns
Soft behind

Dick heaven
Inserted toys
Cock rings
Kitty pleaser

The Moist Prophecy for Sexual Scriptures

My qualifications may be a little higher than your sexual experience. However, I would like to introduce your tongue to my sanctuary and my flamingo or my pink paradise. I'm still a little hesitant as it seems like my experience outshines your current plan but I do see potential in your mission statement so let's collide our bodies to create a growth plan.

Let me paint a naked picture in your mind, so I can go further to rub against your body and then let your spirit be at rest so I can satisfy your soul for days therefore executing tears of satisfaction, joy from a great and sweaty sensual session.

Relax, while I begin to lick the chocolate drop falling from the strawberries on your chest. You switch places with me, place your plate on my ass and eat your peach slices. Go on and squeeze the orange slices on my breast and slurp it off my breast slowly with emphasis on my nipples. You can tease my thick and round lips with those pure yellow bananas before I take the main course.

We can get away from the world and lay on the beach to breathe fresh air while I'm feeding you juicy purple or green grapes. How about i dip my finger into a white chocolate fondue and have you lick it off slowly. Then again, I can simply use my tongue to scoop up some ice cream and have you lick the ice cream off my tongue.

Maybe you can lay me across the kitchen counter and eat the fruit salad off of me. How nice it will be to French kiss you with the taste of fondue with a kick of an apple brandy. We could take it to another level and have you dip your magic stick in caramel and having me lick it off slowly.

I can cover the cap of your tool with whipped cream like it's an ice cream on a cone. Go ahead and explore my sensitive sides with some honey- dipped marshmallows. If you need to see me wet right now maybe you can sit and watch me squeeze each fruit on myself. Then you can just watch me slowly swipe each fruit against my wet walls and eat each fruit slowly with so much passion while you beat off your tool. If you are up for the challenge you can intimidate my tonsils with your chocolate covered tool making it taste like heaven and the cream filling from the chocolate melts gently on my mouth.

Leave my mouth filled with sweet juices before you dive in my career center for the main course, I'll have you working non- stop and you may have to pull an overnight shift. You must abide by the sexual scriptures on the path to satisfying my temple and with this powerful weapon I possess, my duty is to lay it on you extensively and heavily.

Confessions of a Sinful Capricorn

At times I want to explore each and every colour in my box. Each colour is a pleasure unit that executes the ultimate satisfaction. I have to make sure all pleasure units are registered and delivered to their destination. For the foreplay I could stick to a regular dirty devil red in hopes it leaves me breathless and gasping for more.

For my oral pleasure I would like to use the sinful blue which is refreshing whenever and wherever I decide to execute that mouth watering project. I'm an open book to trying something new and out of this world.

The Yummy Yellow is for when I feel the need to be left sticky and sweet. This is when I allow chocolate, whipped cream and more sweet stuff to come into the bedroom. Giving your taste buds a new sensation that will give a kick to your pleasure resume. After all they say the experienced ones have the most fun and reoccurring invitations.

Forbidden Scriptures   Biodun Abudu

I love precious stones and with every precious stone I want to have it my way and they of course have their prices, the higher the better for me. I call upon the diamonds so we can have passionate but Godly sex leaving the heavens to shiver. The emeralds are so I can explore my talents by posing in different positions stretching my legs, hands and resting against the green trees in the forest. The rubies are fiery bangers that define "pain is pleasure", the affliction of the pain leaves you wanting more with the cuffs, chains, whips and spikes to accessorize a memorable moment. The sapphires are to produce timeless never ending action under a gold plated roof leaving us drenched with our sweat.

Click click flash, I'm so picture perfect so before you suggest anything I already dropped my layers on the floor for easier access, making this photoshoot more pleasurable. Would you like to zoom into my temple or maybe dive into it without a plate either way it doesn't matter because it is mandatory you do so before you step further into this juicy atmosphere.

A Capricorn like myself pleads guilty to phonography but that's nothing compared to me being a free

Forbidden Scriptures   Biodun Abudu

bitch in a lace and leather affair and all major condoms are accepted in this facility. My sidekick is always available for a circus affair but you have got to be big, bold and bad. Wise enough to connect the dots and strong enough to break down the walls of that honey cum she possesses.

The Sinful Capricorn in me always has a major plan to take over the world just by getting naked after all I'm not ashamed of my beauty. I'm the reason why the world, certain institutions have dress codes because I'm just pure sex, showing nothing but smooth skin and with every statement I make I am completely honest and completely naked.

I'm always on a mission to satisfying your visual appetite that's why when I am around your vicinity I let my body air dry whenever I step out from a steamy shower. I'm always up for a business deal after all my body is the business center that possess the essential contracts that your company desires but of course I have to make sure I make a grand decision on who I sign a business deal with.

I am yet to meet that historical figure that will take over my private and posh paradise, dipping into my soul mentally and physically putting my head on the ground and my feet in the cloud. You can style your future with me and wrap your body around mine creating a fabulous body trend and we can enjoy each season like the Go Deeper Summer, Let Loose Winter, So Sexual Fall and the Touch Me Softly Spring. Life is like a runway so feel free to walk into my dimension repeatedly and share the intense thrill of a sinful Capricorn like me.

Thank you so much for being open to reading this book. I hope you enjoyed reading it as much as I enjoyed writing it.

You can view more of my work on my website at www.BiodunAbudu.com

Feel free to write me at info@biodunabudu.com

Acknowledgments

A special thanks to the following people:

Carol Tietsworth

Henry Jimenez

Bibi Luz Lozano

You all made this poetry collection possible !

ABOUT THE AUTHOR

Biodun Abudu was born in Rhode Island, but comes from a Nigerian background. He wrote his first title "Tales of My Skin" also based on a true life story in 2011. He then released his second title "Stolen Sanity" in 2019 which is also based on a true life story. When he is not writing, he works as an Artist. In 2011, he graduated with an A.S. degree in Fashion Design, and a B.A. in Merchandising Management with an emphasis on Fashion Merchandising. He currently resides in New York City.

Email : Info@BiodunAbudu.com

Website : www.BiodunAbudu.com

Made in the USA
Columbia, SC
17 September 2022